Say What You See

Family

Rebecca Rissman

Raintree

Chicago, Illinois

Edited by Rebecca Rissman, Daniel Nunn, and Catherine Veitch
Designed by Philippa Jenkins
Picture research by Ruth Blair
Production by Victoria Fitzgerald
Originated by Capstone Global Library

Printed in China

16 15 14 13 12
10 9 8 7 6 5 4 3 2 1

Library of Congress Cataloging-in-Publication Data
Rissman, Rebecca.
Family / Rebecca Rissman.
p. cm.—(Say What You See)
Includes bibliographical references and index.
ISBN 978-1-4109-5048-2 (hb)—ISBN 978-1-4109-5053-6 (pb)—
1. Families—Juvenile literature. I. Title.
HQ744.R568 2013
306.85—dc23   2012011722

Acknowledgments
We would like to thank the following for permission to reproduce
photographs: iStockphoto pp. 13 (© Pavel Losevsky), 16 (©
kristian sekulic), 20 (© Chuck Schmidt); Shutterstock pp. title
page (© Rob Marmion), 4 (© privilege), 5 (© wavebreakmedia
ltd, © Monkey Business Images), 6 (© Kzenon), 7 (©
wavebreakmedia ltd, © Rob Marmion, © Yuri Arcurs), 8 (©
IrinaK, © Anatoliy Samara), 9 (© Monkey Business Images), 10
(© Monkey Business Images), 11 (© Gemenacom, © Monkey
Business Images), 12 (© Karen Struthers), 13 (© Monkey
Business Images), 14 (© wavebreakmedia ltd), 15 (© Dmitriy
Shironosov, © Monkey Business Images, © BlueOrange Studio),
16 (© thieury), 17 (© Kruchankova Maya, © Poznyakov), 18
(© Gorilla), 19 (© UbjsP, © Rdaniel), 20 (© Monkey Business
Images), 21 (© Andrew L.), 22 (© Monkey Business Images, ©
Phase4Photography).

Cover photograph of a family reproduced with permission of
Shutterstock (© Monkey Business Images).

Every effort has been made to contact copyright holders of
material reproduced in this book. Any omissions will be rectified
in subsequent printings if notice is given to the publisher.

Contents

What are these families doing?
Say what you see!

Talking

Cooking

Eating

playing

Puzzling

Cleaning

Washing

Gardening

Watering

Driving

Riding

Walking

Running

Reading

Being Silly

Learning

Watching

Traveling

Splashing

Sightseeing

Rushing

Relaxing

Creating

Painting

Racing

Throwing

Skating

Sharing

Caring

Arguing

21

Hugging

Laughing

22

Can you find these things in the book? Look back . . . and say what you see!

riding

washing

building

caring

Index